MATH YOU WILL A...

MW01153829

USING MATH IN
FINANCE

RICHARD BARRINGTON

rosen publishing's
**rosen
central**®

NEW YORK

Published in 2018 by The Rosen Publishing Group, Inc.
29 East 21st Street, New York, NY 10010

First Edition

Library of Congress Cataloging-in-Publication Data

Names: Barrington, Richard, 1961–
Title: Using math in finance / Richard Barrington.
Description: New York : Rosen Central, 2018. | Series: Math you will actually use | Audience: Grades 5–8. | Includes bibliographical references and index.
Identifiers: LCCN 2016055896| ISBN 9781499438642 (pbk. book) | ISBN 9781499438659 (6 pack) | ISBN 9781499438666 (library bound book)
Subjects: LCSH: Business mathematics—Juvenile literature. | Finance—Mathematical models—Juvenile literature.
Classification: LCC HF5691 .B427 2018 | DDC 332.01/51—dc23
LC record available at https://lccn.loc.gov/2016055896

Manufactured in the United States of America

METRIC CONVERSION CHART	
1 inch = 2.54 centimeters; 25.4 millimeters	1 cup = 250 milliliters
1 foot = 30.48 centimeters	1 ounce = 28 grams
1 yard = .914 meters	1 fluid ounce = 30 milliliters
1 square foot = .093 square meters	1 teaspoon = 5 milliliters
1 square mile = 2.59 square kilometers	1 tablespoon = 15 milliliters
1 ton = .907 metric tons	1 quart = .946 liters
1 pound = 454 grams	355 degrees Fahrenheit = 180 degrees Celsius
1 mile = 1.609 kilometers	

CONTENTS

INTRODUCTION

"Why do I have to learn math?"

Plenty of students have asked that question at some point in their education. Doing division, calculating numbers out to several decimal points, or solving for x might not seem like tasks that matter much in the real world. However, those skills come into play all the time when handling one very important part of life: money.

A ten-year old eyeing a candy bar in a supermarket must count the nickels in his pocket to see if he has enough to buy the candy. Meanwhile, as the head of a large corporation thinks about spending billions of dollars to buy another company, she must look at a number of calculations to figure out whether it is worth it. These situations have two things in common: they both matter a great deal to the person involved and they both require using math to arrive at an answer.

People use math to deal with money all the time. Adults generally earn a paycheck, have bank accounts, and pay bills. All the things that affect how people handle their money are known as personal finance. Making good decisions about personal finance depends on math skills. Without those skills, how would people know how much they could afford to spend or whether an investment was a good idea?

Beyond that, many jobs involve numbers. Whether it is measuring the size of a suit or planning the budget for a big corporation, numbers are a central part of many professions. Thus, students today can expect that when they grow up they will be dealing with numbers in both their personal lives and their jobs.

Actually, using math to manage personal finances becomes a bigger part of a person's life as they grow up, and chances are by the time kids are out of elementary school they are already using some math when they handle money. For example, if a boy goes into a store and gives the cashier a dollar bill for a 75 cent candy bar, he probably knows to expect a quarter back in change. Without even thinking that he is using math, this boy has used subtraction to figure out the difference between a dollar and seventy-five cents.

The point is, students are probably already using math skills in personal finance whenever they handle money. This book is designed to help them build on those skills, by explaining how specific types of math may be used in personal finance now and when they grow up.

All of this demonstrates a big reason students need to learn math—their money depends on it. Anyone who does not want to waste money needs to learn the math skills necessary to handle it wisely.

CHAPTER 1

Breaking It Down: How Money Comes in Fractions

Before looking at how to perform mathematical operations like addition and subtraction with money, a good place to start is by understanding how to use fractions when dealing with money. After all, prices posted throughout a store are rarely expressed in whole dollars. Look at a handful of coins, and each represents some portion of a dollar. Because amounts of money usually aren't round dollar figures, it is necessary to deal with them in fractions, and fractions expressed in decimal terms.

FRACTIONS OF DOLLARS

In everyday conversation, people are used to amounts of money being expressed in fractions. For example, a person might refer to the amount $2.50 as "two-and-a-half dollars"

The name of a common coin, the quarter, is an example of how fractions relate to money. The name represents the fraction of a dollar the coin is worth.

rather than saying "two dollars and fifty cents."

Coins help deal with fractions of dollars. They allow people to break a dollar up into smaller portions so money can be exchanged for the exact cost of a product, rather than rounded to the nearest dollar. After all, it would be unfair if every time someone bought something worth seventy-five cents they had to pay a full dollar and did not get any change back.

The name of one coin, the quarter, provides a clear example of how coins are designed to represent fractions of dollars. The amount the quarter represents, 25 cents, is one-quarter of a dollar. Though the names of other coins don't coincide quite as clearly with the fractions of dollars they represent, the value of each is designed to represent a particular fraction of a dollar.

Fractions are easy to deal with when a number can be broken into a few even pieces, such as the way a dollar can be broken into four quarters. However, fractions get messier when numbers are not so evenly broken down. For example, for $1.65 it would be awkward to write "1 and 65/100 dollars" or say "one dollar and sixty-five one-hundredths of a dollar." To make things easier, fractions of dollars are usually expressed in decimal terms.

CENTS AS DECIMALS

The word "cent" comes from the Latin word *centum* meaning "hundred." Every cent is worth one-hundredth of a dollar, or 1/100 dollar. In decimal terms, that fraction can be converted to $0.01.

When it comes to more complex mathematical operations, decimals are much easier to deal with than fractions. So, while a quarter is 1/4 of a dollar, its value is usually expressed in decimal terms, as $0.25. This makes it easier to add on other amounts that may have different denominations. For example, an odd number like 37 cents would make an awkward looking fraction, but expressed in decimal terms as $0.37 it is readily added to other amounts, as in $0.37 plus $0.25 equals $0.62.

Of course, when such numbers reach 100 cents they become whole dollars. This is how amounts of money are usually expressed, in terms of the whole number of dollars and then a decimal fraction representing the additional number of cents.

Knowing what fractions of a dollar a coin represents can be helpful when counting money because it shows how to convert multiple coins to dollars. The cash drawers at stores or banks will

Coins take up a lot of space. But coin roll wrappers organize large numbers of coins into neat packages of uniform values. This helps stores and banks count their coins easily.

TRY IT YOURSELF: WHAT FRACTION OF A DOLLAR ARE THESE COINS?

The name of the quarter directly refers to what fraction of a dollar that coin represents, but though they may not be labeled quite as clearly, other coins also represent a specific fraction of a dollar.

Think of some common coins—a penny, a nickel, and a dime. What fraction of a dollar does each one represent? To figure this out, you can start by showing the value of each as a fraction of the one hundred cents that make up a dollar. For example, since a quarter is worth twenty-five cents, it is 25/100 of a dollar. That fraction can then be simplified to 1/4, and as noted previously, a quarter gets its name from the fact that it represents one quarter of a dollar.

1a. Try that with the other coins: express the penny, nickel, and dime as fractions of a dollar and then reduce them to their simplest fraction.

1b. Next, add different kinds of coins. For example, what fraction of a dollar would one quarter, one nickel, and three dimes represent when added together?

often have coins bundled into rolls made up of a specific number of those coins. By knowing the number of coins in each roll and what fraction of a dollar those coins represent, a cashier can readily figure out how much that roll of coins is worth without having to take the money out and count it.

PERFORMING MATHEMATICAL OPERATIONS WITH MONEY

Since a penny is the lowest denomination in US money, one could avoid fractions and decimals altogether by expressing amounts in terms of the number of cents rather than dollars. This is often done with relatively small amounts of money. For example, on a price sign in a store something costing $0.65 might simply be labeled as "65 cents," or "65¢."

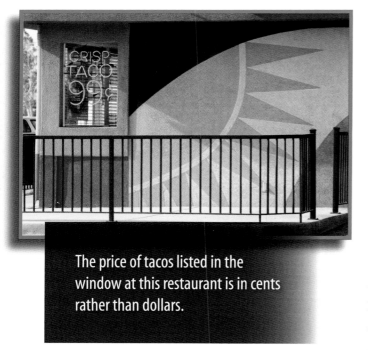

The price of tacos listed in the window at this restaurant is in cents rather than dollars.

That approach is fine until it comes to dealing with much larger sums. Think of someone with a salary of $50,000. That is the equivalent of 5,000,000 cents. It is less awkward to talk about numbers like this in terms of dollars than as a huge amount of pennies.

This book will show examples of mathematical operations with amounts of money expressed both in cents and in dollars. However, since showing things in dollar terms with cents representing a decimal fraction of a dollar is more common, most of the examples in this book will take the approach of using dollar terms.

CHAPTER 2

ADDITION AND SUBTRACTION: MAKING AND SPENDING MONEY

Addition and subtraction are the basic building blocks of math, and in a similar way they are also the building blocks of finance. Finance involves managing the process of making and spending money. Addition and subtraction are used to keep track of money being earned and money being spent.

KEEPING TRACK OF A BANK ACCOUNT

If someone puts all their money out on a table in front of them, they could simply count it to see how much they have. Of course, keeping their money with them at all times would also make it easy to have that money stolen, or damaged by flood or fire. Protecting money is one reason people use bank accounts.

Addition and subtraction help banks and their customers keep track of how much an account has. These operations occur when various amounts have been deposited and withdrawn.

With a bank account, the bank keep tracks of how much money their customers put in and how much they take out, and the remainder is known as the balance. That balance represents the amount of money the customer has left. However, it is not enough to have the bank keep track of an account's balance. After all, banks sometimes make mistakes, and customers need to be aware of how much they have left in the account even before getting updated information from the bank.

Fortunately, addition and subtraction make it easy to keep track of how much money is in a bank account. Money going into the account, which is known as a deposit, would be added to the balance. Money taken out, which is known as a withdrawal, would be subtracted from the balance.

MANAGING SAVINGS AND EXPENSES

Addition and subtraction can do more than just keep track of what has already happened. They also make it possible to plan for the fu-

ACCOUNTING: ADDING AND SUBTRACTING FOR A LIVING

While simple addition and subtraction can be used to keep track of deposits and withdrawals and plan for expenses, this quickly becomes more complicated when dealing with a business that has deposits coming in from many sources and also has a large number of bills to pay, from employee paychecks to rent on the office to the cost of supplies.

Accounting can be a rewarding profession that makes use of the math skills necessary to keep track of money.

Keeping track of business finances can quickly become a full-time job. It would be hard to do that and have any time to spend on the main duties of running a business, such as managing people and deciding what to sell.

That is why there are accountants, professionals who specialize in helping people and businesses keep track of their money. Accountants don't just add and subtract money going in and out of an account. They also might figure out how much tax the business owes and how fast a business might grow.

People who are good at math and enjoy solving problems might consider accounting as a career. A good first step is to look for opportunities to get into advanced math classes.

TRY IT YOURSELF—HOW MUCH MONEY WILL YOU HAVE LEFT?

It's exciting to receive money as a gift. Knowing financial math can help plan how to use that money.

Long before you start earning a paycheck and have to pay household bills, you can use addition and subtraction to plan ahead for how to spend the money you receive as gifts or allowance.

Suppose someone gives you $30 for your birthday. You want to go to an amusement park with friends at the end of the month in four weeks, and you know this will cost $25. In the meantime, you will receive $6 per week for doing chores around the house. Next week, you want to go to a movie that costs $7.50.

2. If you also decide to splurge on a 75 cent bag of potato chips once per week, how much money will this leave you at the end of the month, after the trip to the amusement park?

ture. This is a key part of finance because it allows people to figure out whether they will have enough money to meet all the expenses they expect to have.

One way to manage this is with a budget. Suppose Kate earns $1,000 per week. She spends $75 per week on groceries, $1,200 per month on her rent, and $60 per month on her electric bill. Those are her most important bills, the ones she wants to make sure she can pay before she spends any other money. Since a month is roughly four weeks, she can expect her paychecks during a month to make four additions of $1,000 each to her bank account. However, over those same four weeks she will also spend $75 each week on groceries. That will add up to $300 in a month. At the end of the month, Kate will also have to pay $1,200 in rent and $60 for the electric bill.

Looking a month ahead then, Kate can expect to see $4,000 added to her account, but then four subtractions of $75, as well as subtractions of $1,200 and $60. That leaves $2,440. Based on this, Kate knows that she has a budget of $2,440 that she can either spend on other things or save.

Understanding math principles as simple as adding and subtracting can make finance less complicated than it might seem at first. Math students are taught to break a long equation into smaller operations and do them one by one to simplify the equation. In a similar way, finance might involve a large number of transactions, but those transactions each typically involve a relatively simple mathematical operation if approached step by step.

CHAPTER 3

Watching Money Grow Through Multiplication

Addition and subtraction can handle the most basic types of financial transactions, such as receiving and spending money. Often though, the operations involved are more complex, or it would simply be faster to multiply a large number of identical transactions rather than add or subtract them over and over again. This is why multiplication is useful in finance.

BUYING IN BULK

Consider some examples one might see on a typical trip to the grocery store. Suppose corn on the cob is selling for 50 cents an ear. Joe wants to buy 12 ears for a cookout he is having, but he only has $7.00 in his pocket. He would like to know if that is enough before he brings them to checkout.

Joe could use addition and add 50 cents together 12 times to arrive at his total, but that is time consuming and it is easy to lose track when doing something so repetitive. It would be much more straightforward for Joe to use multiplication.

Since Joe would have to spend 50 cents 12 times over to buy all the corn he wants, he can multiply 50 cents by 12 to figure out what the total cost would be. The answer is 600 cents. This converts to $6.00, so with seven dollars in his pocket, Joe has enough money with a dollar to spare.

Multiplication can also help figure out when it is cheaper to buy in bulk. For example, suppose individual bottles of soda are selling for a dollar each, but a six-pack is selling for $5.00. Multiplying one dollar by six shows that it would cost $6.00 to buy that much soda in individual bottles, so the six-pack does represent a money-saving deal.

TRY IT YOURSELF—IS THIS A GOOD DEAL?

A store will often label prices in multiple quantities to try to get people to buy more. For example, a bakery might sell three large chocolate chip cookies for $2.00. Assuming that this is a special price that applied only for buying cookies three at a time may be wrong. Ask how much it would cost to buy a single cookie, and the baker will say that they cost 75 cents each.

3. Which is the better deal?

Stores may sell items individually or bundled together. Multiplication can help a shopper figure out which is the better deal.

TIME AND MONEY

Multiplication is especially useful when it comes to showing how a regular payment of money would add up over time. For example, suppose Juan had a job making $1,250 per week. Multiplying that by fifty-two weeks, he could figure out that he was making $65,000 per year. Sometimes wages are expressed as an annual salary instead of a weekly amount. If Juan were offered another job paying $75,000 per year, being able to convert his current weekly salary to an annual rate would let him compare the wages of the two jobs.

Multiplication also helps when people are trying to save money. Landon and Abby are a married couple who have found they can save $300 per month out of their combined pay. By multiplying by 12 they could figure out that they would save $3,600 over the course of a year. They could further multiply that $3,600 by five to figure out that they would save $18,000 in five years. This

MULTIPLYING MONEY FOR THE FUTURE—FINANCIAL PLANNING AS A CAREER

The example of Landon and Abby is a fairly simple projection of savings over a limited period of time. When people think about their financial futures though, things get more complicated. There are often multiple things to save for, increases in prices to worry about, and the possibility of making different amounts of money in the future.

Financial planners help people figure out how much money they will need for the future, and how to save and invest to build up that amount of money. Multiplication is at the heart of the calculations about the future that financial planners do. People who like using math to solve problems and are good at explaining math to others might want to consider a career in financial planning.

Big purchases like a car require careful planning. Financial planners use math skills to help people make major decisions about their money.

would be useful information if they were trying to save for a down payment on a house or to send their kids to college.

Multiplication does more than help figure out how fast a person can make or save money. It can also show how much something will cost in the long run if that cost is expressed as monthly payments.

For example, Big Lou's Used Cars might be advertising a family sedan for sale at "just $199 per month." $199 might sound very affordable, but multiplying that out shows how much the car will really cost. $199 per month for a year would cost twelve times that, or $2,388. If it turns out those payments went on for seven years, you would multiply $2,388 by seven to find the eventual total cost would be $16,716. The car may or may not be worth that, but in any case it is a long way from "just $199."

CHAPTER 4

Cutting Things Down to Size with Division

Division is multiplication in reverse, so just as multiplication can show how money will accumulate, division can break down larger numbers to show what they would represent over smaller periods of time or purchase quantities.

PRICING AND PAYMENT STRATEGIES

Division can be used to break larger sums of money down into standard amounts for comparison purposes. Two examples of this are when prices vary for different quantities of a product, and when calculating annual pay on a monthly, weekly, or hourly basis.

For example, the dairy department at the supermarket might be selling a gallon of milk for $3.40 per gallon, while one-quart containers of the same type of milk are selling for $0.95 each. This is often the case even within the same name brand. Since there are four quarts in a gallon, dividing the gallon price by four allows it to be compared to the one-quart price. In this case, buying milk by

FIGURING OUT HOW TO TURN A PROFIT

It is often cheaper overall to buy things in large quantities than one at a time, and this is the basis for how supermarkets and other retail stores make a profit.

Warren Buffett, one of the world's richest men, has made billions running several different businesses, but he started his first when he was just six years old. Back then, he was able to buy a six-pack of soda for 25 cents. He then sold the cans individually for a nickel apiece. Dividing the six-pack price of 25 cents by six shows that Buffet was paying just over four cents per can for the soda he bought. By then selling it for five cents per can, he was making nearly a penny's profit for each can.

Running a business is a little more complicated than that. Besides the cost of goods being sold, there are employees, rent, and advertising to be paid for. And yet, the general principle of determining pricing based on cost per unit is one of the building blocks for turning a profit. This is something useful to remember for anyone who wants to manage a retail business as a career.

Things like milk are sold in several different sizes of containers. A gallon of milk may cost less per ounce than a pint.

the gallon costs $0.85 per quart, or ten cents less per quart than buying milk one quart at a time.

Besides helping to figure out how much things cost per unit, division can help people better understand how much the money they earn represents when measured over different time periods.

For example, people's first jobs are generally paid on an hourly basis, but for more experienced employees jobs often pay a salary—an annual rate of pay. Division is useful for breaking that annual rate down to show people how much they are making over a shorter period of time.

One reason this is useful is that most of the bills people pay, like for rent, electricity, and phone plans, are charged on a monthly basis. If someone had a salary of $48,000 per year, dividing that total by twelve would show that it meant earning $4,000 per month. Knowing that would be the starting point for figuring out a monthly budget of how much that person could afford to spend.

TRY IT YOURSELF—HOW MUCH ARE YOU REALLY MAKING?

Suppose you had a full-time job making $15 an hour, and got offered a job working the same schedule but at an annual salary of $25,000.

    4. Assuming you would have a 40-hour workweek and 50 weeks of work during the year (leaving two weeks for vacation) at both jobs, would the new offer be better or worse than your current job?

BUDGETING FOR PURCHASES AND SAVINGS

A common way of using division to break a large amount down into smaller pieces is to figure out how long it would take to accumulate a targeted amount of money.

    For example, Tony wants to save up for a skateboard that costs $35. By doing jobs around the house and yard and by spending as little money as possible, he finds he can save $5 per week. By dividing the total he needs by the rate of savings, he can tell how many weeks it will take him to afford the skateboard. In this case, $35 divided by $5 works out to seven weeks of saving before Tony can afford the skateboard.

Divide the price of a purchase into the periodic earnings of allowance. This calculation can help kids figure out how long they would have to do household chores before they can buy an expensive item.

Division can also be used to help plan for longer-term goals, like retirement. Suppose Jack and Meg decide they want to have $500,000 by the time they retire in 25 years. That may sound like an impossible amount of money to accumulate, but by using division Jack and Meg can break that amount into more manageable increments. $500,000 divided by 25 years comes to $20,000 per year. Divided by 52 weeks, that would mean Jack and Meg would have to accumulate about $384.62 in savings and investment earnings per week. That gives them a more manageable goal they can try to work into their weekly budget.

CHAPTER 5

PUTTING FINANCES IN PERSPECTIVE WITH PERCENTAGES

Percentages are important to finance because they show the size of one number in relation to another. For example, if A is 50% of B, then it is clear that B is twice as big as A without having to know the actual amounts that A and B represent. In finance, this allows people to apply a given percentage relationship between numbers to a variety of situations.

DISCOUNTS

A common way the use of percentages can be observed when shopping is the way sales are often advertised. For example, something may be advertised as 30% off. But what does that really mean?

This store is having a sale. Knowing how to use percentages can help with figuring out the exact dollar value of the discounted items.

A percentage represents a portion of another number. In decimal terms, thirty percent equals 0.30 times the other number. Therefore, to find the value of a 30% discount, one would multiply the normal price by 0.30. Since the result represents the amount of the discount, that could then be subtracted from the normal price to see how much the item would cost if bought on sale.

For example, if something normally costs $10 and is selling for 30% off, the discount would be 0.30 • $10, or $3. Subtracting this from $10 would result in a sale price of $7.

Using percentages to represent a discount has two benefits. One is that it gives a sense of scale for how big a discount is relative to the normal price. For example, a 5% discount would represent only a slight savings, while a 40% discount means that a significant portion of the original price is being taken off.

The other benefit is being able to apply the same rate of discount to multiple quantities. Take the earlier case of a $10 item on sale for 30% off. Suppose a person wanted to buy five of those items. How much would the discount amount to, and what would be the total cost? Buying five items at a price of $10 would cost $50. Multiplying

TRY IT YOURSELF—WHICH DISCOUNT IS BETTER?

Some discounts are advertised in percentage terms, while some are advertised in dollar terms. Being able to convert percentages to dollars allows you to compare which is a better deal.

5. Suppose one store advertised $30 jeans on sale for 25% off. Another store offered a $10 off coupon for the same $30 jeans. Which is the better deal?

that by 0.30 results in a discount of $15. Subtracting the discount from the normal price results in a sale cost of $35.

INTEREST RATES AND COMPOUNDING

Another common way percentages are used in finance is to represent interest rates. Interest rates are an amount of money a person earns for letting another person use their money for a while. If Mickey lends Bill $10, there is a risk that Bill might not pay him back. Also, in the meantime Mickey does not have use of that $10. To reward Mickey for the risk and the inconvenience of letting Bill use his money, Bill might agree to give Mickey more than $10 when he pays the money back. The extra money is a rate of interest, and it is generally expressed as the percentage of extra money that would be earned over the course of one year.

This can work both ways for consumers. When they deposit money in a savings account at a bank, they are letting the bank use their money while it is in there. In return, the customer earns interest. For example, a 1% interest rate on a $1,000 deposit would earn 0.01 • $1,000, or $10, over the course of a year.

On the other hand, when consumers borrow money from a bank, they pay interest. A $1,000 home loan might cost a customer 4%. Therefore, the customer could expect to pay interest at a rate of 0.04 • $1,000, or $40 per year.

A final important thing to understand about interest is compounding. Compounding magnifies the impact of interest rates over longer periods of time, because once interest is earned that interest can then start earning more interest.

Earning ten percent interest on $100 would produce $10 in interest the first year (0.10 • $100). That would make the total $110. Earning the same rate of interest the second year would produce $11 (0.10 • $110). Because of compounding, the interest earned the second year is greater, even though the interest rate remained the same.

Interest rates are measured in percentages. These rates show how much the value of an account, whether it's savings or a loan, will grow.

HOW BANKS MAKE MONEY

In the examples given for how interest rates work, note that the percentage interest that a consumer would have earned for depositing money was less than the percentage that would be charged for taking out a loan.

While these percentages may vary, it is generally the case that banks charge more for lending money than they pay people for depositing money with them. This is part of how banks make money. Of course, banks have to pay for things like security and the risk that people might not repay their loans, but generally the difference in the interest rates they set on loans and deposits is designed to earn them a profit. This difference is often known as "the spread."

Students who want to learn about possible careers in banking should learn their percentages well, and later on take courses in economics to understand how things like inflation and unemployment might affect interest rates.

Compounding matters because the longer a person deposits money without withdrawing any, the more interest that money can earn. For the same reason, the longer a person borrows money without making payments on the loan, the more interest it will cost because of compounding.

CHAPTER 6

GETTING THE ANSWER BY SOLVING FOR VARIABLES

Sometimes, a key piece of information is missing from an equation, and a variable, serving as a placeholder, represents it. When that happens, different mathematical operations may be used to figure out the missing piece of information based on what is known. This is called solving for a variable.

FIGURING OUT THE UNKNOWN

There are two stages to using variables to answer financial questions. One is to set up an equation that represents the known fixed values and what the missing piece of information, or variable, is. The other is then to isolate that missing piece of information so it can be calculated by performing the inverse operations on the known information.

Variables are often represented by the letter x. One example is in the equation $2 + 3 = x$. However, sometimes a different component of the equation might be the unknown. For example, an equation might be presented as $2 + x = 5$. The total, 5, and one of the components of the equation, 2, are fixed values because they are numbers. To solve for x and find the variable, do whatever inverse operation the situation requires to all sides of the equation. Multiplication and division are inverse operations of each other, addition and subtraction are inverse operations of each other, and exponents and logarithms/power functions are the inverse operations of each other (but personal finance for minors generally has little to do with these more complicated types of equations). To isolate x with the inverse operation required in $2 + x = 5$ (the meaning is the same when this equation is written as "$x + 2 = 5$"), subtract 2 from both sides to discover that $x = 3$.

Working with variables is often necessary in finance. A person might know what the desired end result is, but needs to figure out what financial actions will lead to that result. For example, if Stevie wants to buy a sweatshirt that costs $30 and would like to have it by the time he goes back to school in five weeks, he can work backward from the end goal ($30) to find out how much he will have to save every week to meet that goal.

The question Stevie is trying to answer is what amount multiplied over five weeks would equal $30. The equation in this case would look like this: $5x = \$30$. That is because Stevie knows he is dealing with five weeks and that he wants to end up with $30. Having put this in the form of an equation, Stevie would isolate the x variable by dividing both sides by 5 because division is the inverse operation of multiplication. The result is that $x = \$6$.

TRY IT YOURSELF—HOW LONG BEFORE YOU CAN AFFORD IT?

Suppose you want to buy a $24 baseball cap and you think you can save $2 per week for it.

6a. How long would it take for you to save the amount you need?

6b. How long would it take if you saved $3 per week?

BUDGETING AND SAVING

Solving for variables comes up in a number of budgeting and saving situations. Sometimes, the goal is to figure out how much a person can afford to spend. For example, if Chrissie earns $1,000 per week and has certain fixed expenses like rent and a car payment, she might wonder how much she could afford to spend on day-to-day expenses like food and entertainment.

Assume that she will get four weekly paychecks in the typical month and pays $850 in rent and $300 for her car payment. Chrissie wants to know how much more she can spend

Paying bills is a predictable part of budgeting because bills arrive pretty regularly in the mail.

before she runs out of money. She could set an equation up this way: $(4 \cdot \$1,000) - \$850 - \$300 - x = \$0$. This shows her four paychecks, her regular monthly bills, and an unknown spending amount

HOW INVESTMENT ANALYSTS MAKE DECISIONS

For people who like math, figuring out the value of an unknown variable can be like solving a puzzle. In finance, those puzzles can get extremely complex. For some, that makes solving financial puzzles a challenging and rewarding career.

Financial analysts often work with long, complicated equations that may have changeable parts. The answers they are seeking might represent what profit a company might make if it takes certain actions, or whether the interest generated from a loan might be greater than the cost of making the loan.

People who are interested in this kind of career should seek out courses that give them a good background in both math and business, and generally should expect to go to graduate school after college to earn an advanced degree like a Masters of Business Administration (MBA).

that would leave her with no money at the end of the month. Solving for x, Chrissie would find that $x = \$2,850$. That's how much she can afford to spend without living beyond her means. If she wanted to start saving money, Chrissie could choose to spend an amount less than \$2,850, but more than the \$1,150 of her fixed expenses.

Solving for unknown variables is also an important part of retirement saving. These are complicated calculations because they include things like investment returns and inflation, but basically they involve working backward to solve for an unknown amount. If a person knows how much money they want to have in retirement and how many years of work they have left, they can set up an equation to solve for the amount of money they will need to save every year to meet that target.

CONCLUSION

At an age when kids are first given money of their own to spend, they begin to face decisions about money. Learning math can help them make better decisions with money. Math can help kids understand what is the best deal when they are shopping, and it can help them figure out how to save up for a big purchase.

From the time kids first start earning an allowance, they need to use math skills to understand how to get the most out of their money.

As kids grow into adults, the numbers get larger and the financial decisions get more complicated, but the same skills still apply. For those who have an interest and talent in math, this knowledge can even become a career in finance. Careers in the field include accounting, financial planning, business management, banking, and investment analysis. All are fields in which there are many jobs that tend to pay above-average salaries.

People with a solid understanding of math will be better informed as consumers and more prepared to make important decisions about things like living on a budget and saving for retirement. The ability to do this can help with living a better lifestyle.

ANSWERS

Answer 1a. One penny = 1/100 of a dollar; a nickel = 5/100 = 1/20 of a dollar; a dime = 10/100 = 1/10 of a dollar.

Answer 1b. One quarter's value is $.25, or 25/100. A nickel is $.05, or 5/100. It reduces to 1/20. Three dimes is $.30, or 30/100. It reduces to 3/10. These fractions demonstrate that cent values describe some value over 100, so they already have the same denominator. Adding these values (25/100 + 5/100 + 30/100) equals 60/100, or $.60. For simplification's sake, you can reduce this fraction to 3/5 of a dollar.

Answer 2. Set this up as a mathematical equation using addition and subtraction to figure out the answer. Remember that generally speaking, amounts of money that are expressed in cents should be converted to a decimal fraction of a dollar to be combined with amounts expressed in dollars. Remaining money after amusement park = $30 + $6 + $6 + $6 + $6 - $7.50 - $0.75 - $0.75 - $0.75 - $0.75 - $25 = $18.50.

Answer 3. Use multiplication to see how much it would cost to buy three cookies individually. Then, use subtraction to compare that to the 3-for-$2.00 price to see how much that deal would save you, if anything. 3 • 0.75 = $2.25; and then $2.25 - $2.00 = $0.25. The 3-for-$2.00 deal saves Greg 25 cents.

Answer 4. To figure this out, use division to convert the $25,000 annual salary to an hourly rate. Earnings per week =

$25,000/50 weeks = $500 per week. Earnings per hour = $500/40 hours = $12.50 per hour. The new job would not pay as well as the current job.

Answer 5. Convert the percentage sale into a dollar value to find out how much you would save on the jeans. Then compare that to the $10 coupon to decide which store was offering a better deal. Discount = $30 • 0.25 = $7.50 . Since this is less than $10, the store offering the coupon has a better deal on the jeans.

Answer 6a. Set up an equation where x is the number of weeks it will take before you can afford the cap, and $2 is the increment that the equation increases by. Then, solve for x. $2x = $24; x = $24/$2; x = 12 weeks.
Answer 6b. Set up a new equation to see what would happen if you were able to save $3 per week, and find out how much more quickly this would allow you to afford the cap. The equation is: $3x = $24; x = $24/$3; x = 8 weeks.

GLOSSARY

ACCOUNTANT A professional who keeps financial records and checks them to make sure they are accurate and that payments are made and received on time.

BANK ACCOUNT The amount kept at a bank on behalf of a specific customer, available for future use by that customer.

BUDGET A plan for receiving and spending money that helps a person prepare for future needs without overspending.

CASH DRAWER Typically in a cash register, the place where coins and bills are sorted as they are received from customers and kept available to make change.

CASHIER The person in a store who adds the prices of what a customer is buying, receives money in payment for those items and gives the customer change if necessary.

COMPOUNDING When at the end of a period, interest earnings are combined with the principal and previous periods' interest earnings, so that the interest rate is applied to the total amount for greater earnings in each period.

DENOMINATION When dealing with money, this means the amount that a given unit of money represents, e.g., a quarter represents 25 cents, a ten-dollar bill represents ten dollars, etc.

DEPOSIT Money placed in or added to a bank account.

DISCOUNT A reduction in price of something for sale, usually as a special offer.

DOWN PAYMENT Large purchases are often made by borrowing money but generally there also needs to be a certain portion of the price paid up front, which is known as the down payment.

ECONOMICS The study of things that determine how goods are produced and sold, how money is earned and spent, and how these things affect wealth and employment.

FINANCE The business and study of how people and businesses handle decisions about making, spending, and investing money.

FINANCIAL ANALYST Professionals who examine data and make judgements about what outcomes certain financial trends and decisions will have.

FINANCIAL PLANNERS Professionals who advise people on handling their money through saving, spending, and investing.

FULL-TIME JOB This is employment that is expected to provide most or all of a person's income, generally in exchange for working about 40 hours per week.

INTEREST RATE A percentage earned by one party in exchange for giving another party the use of a sum of money which is eventually expected to be paid back with an additional interest amount.

INVERSE OPERATION An operation that does the opposite action as another operation, like multiplying as the inverse if division, or addition as the inverse of subtraction.

PRINCIPAL The amount of money that an institution or individual loans out.

PROJECTION Using what is expected to happen with money flowing in and out to see how much money will be available in the future.

RENT A regular fee paid in exchange for using someone else's property, such as an apartment or a car.

RETIREMENT This is the stage after working for a living, at which point one generally has to live on retirement benefits and/or money saved and invested while working.

SALARY An arrangement whereby an employee is paid a specific amount over a period of time, regardless of how many hours were worked during that period.

TRANSACTION An exchange of money between two or more parties, such as buying something from a store or depositing money in a bank.

WITHDRAWAL Money taken out of a bank account.

FOR MORE INFORMATION

American Institute of Certified Public Accountants
1211 Avenue of the Americas
New York, NY 10036
Website: https://www.aicpa.org
An institute that sets standards for Certified Public Accountants
in the US and advocates on behalf of accountants.

Association for Financial Professionals
4520 East-West Highway, Suite 800
Bethesda, MD 20814
Website: https://www.afponline.org
An organization dedicated to setting standards for and provid-
ing information to finance professionals.

Canadian Institute of Financial Planners
3660 Hurontario Street, Suite 600
Mississauga, ON L5B 3C4
Canada
Website: https://www.cifps.ca
A professional association for financial planners in Canada.

Chartered Financial Analyst Institute
477 Madison Ave #21
New York, NY 10022
Website: https://www.cfainstitute.org
An organization that promotes ethical, educational, and profes-
sional standards in the investment industry.

Chartered Professional Accountants of Canada
277 Wellington St. West
Toronto, ON M5V 3H2
Canada
Website: https://www.cpacanada.ca
A provider of information and professional development programs for accountants in Canada.

National Association of Personal Financial Advisors
8700 W. Bryn Mawr Avenue
Suite 700N
Chicago, IL 60631
Website: https://www.napfa.org
A professional association that sets ethical standards for financial advisors whose fee structures are designed to encourage independent and objective advice.

WEBSITES

Because of the changing nature of internet links, Rosen Publishing has developed an online list of websites related to the subject of this book. This site is updated regularly. Please use this link to access this list:

http://www.rosenlinks.com/MYWAU/finance

FOR FURTHER READING

Andal, Walter. *Finance 101 for Kids: Money Lessons Children Cannot Afford to Miss*. Minneapolis, MN: Mill City Press, 2016.

Bernstein, Daryl. *Better Than a Lemonade Stand! Small Business Ideas for Kids*. New York, NY: Aladdin, 2012.

Bianchi, David W. *Blue Chip Kids: What Every Child (and Parent) Should Know About Money, Investing, and the Stock Market*. Hoboken, NJ: John Wiley & Sons, Inc., 2015.

Furgang, Kathy. *National Geographic Kids Everything Money: A wealth of facts, photos, and fun!* Des Moines, IA: National Geographic Children's Books, 2013.

McGillian, Jamie Kyle. *The Kids' Money Book: Earning, Saving, Spending, Investing, Donating*. New York, NY: Sterling Children's Books, 2016.

McGuire, Kara. *The Teen Money Manual: A Guide to Cash, Credit, Spending, Saving, Work, Wealth, and More*. North Mankato, MN: Capstone Young Readers, 2014.

Reynolds, Mattie. *Kids Making Money: An Introduction to Financial Literacy*. South Egremont, MA: Red Chair Press, 2013.

Scott, Elaine. *Dollars & Sense: A Kid's Guide to Using—Not Losing—Money*. Watertown, MA: Charlesbridge, 2016.

Vermond, Kira. *The Secret Life of Money: A Kid's Guide to Cash*. Markham, ON: Owlkids Books, 2012.

Zimmerman, Bennett. *Go! Stock! Go! A Stock Market Guide for Enterprising Children and their Curious Parents*. Santa Monica, CA: The Fourth Way World, 2014.

BIBLIOGRAPHY

Brown, Steven J., and Mark P. Kritzman. *Quantitative Methods for Financial Analysis*. Homewood, IL: Dow-Jones Irwin, 1987.

Buffett, Warren. "How to teach your kids about money." CNBC, November 22, 2013. http://www.cnbc.com/2013/11/22/buffett-how-to-teach-your-kids-about-moneycommentary.html.

Ellis, Charles D. *Classics: An Investor's Anthology*. Homewood, IL: Dow-Jones Irwin, 1989.

Ellis, Charles D. *Classics II: Another Investor's Anthology*. Homewood, IL: Business One Irwin, 1991.

Ellis, Charles D. *Investment Policy: How to Win the Loser's Game*. Homewood, IL: Dow-Jones Irwin, 1985.

Engel, Louis. *How to Buy Stocks*. New York, NY: Bantam Books, 1980.

Fabozzi, Frank J., and Irving M. Pollack. *The Handbook of Fixed Income Securities*. Homewood, IL: Dow-Jones Irwin, 1987.

IXL. "Math." Retrieved August 17, 2016. https://www.ixl.com/math.

Maginn, John L., and Donald L. Tuttle. *Managing Investment*

Portfolios: A Dynamic Process. Boston, MA: Warren, Gorham & Lamont, 1983.

Shin, Laura. "The 5 Most Important Money Lessons to Teach Your Kids." *Forbes*, October 15, 2013. http://www.forbes.com/sites/laurashin/2013/10/15/the-5-most-important-money-lessons-to-teach-your-kids/2/#5e8727e341a3.

United States Bureau of Labor Statistics. "Accountants and Auditors." December 17, 2015. http://www.bls.gov/ooh/Business-and-Financial/Accountants-and-auditors.htm.

United States Bureau of Labor Statistics. "Financial Analysts." December 17, 2015. http://www.bls.gov/ooh/business-and-financial/financial-analysts.htm.

United States Bureau of Labor Statistics. "Personal Financial Advisors." December 17, 2015. http://www.bls.gov/ooh/business-and-financial/personal-financial-advisors.htm.

United States Consumer Financial Protection Bureau. "Resources for parents: Middle childhood." Retrieved August 17, 2016. http://www.consumerfinance.gov/money-as-you-grow/middle-childhood.

INDEX

ABOUT THE AUTHOR

In over twenty years with an investment advisory firm, Richard Barrington's roles included heading marketing and client service as well as participating in investment policy and executive committees. For the past several years Barrington has been a financial writer and has had material syndicated on MSN.com, the Huffington Post, and Forbes.com. He has also appeared on National Public Radio's *Talk of the Nation*, American Public Media's *Marketplace*, and Fox Business News. He graduated from St. John Fisher College with a BA in communications and earned his chartered financial analyst designation from the CFA Institute.

PHOTO CREDITS